I love quotes, they provide a quick hit of inspiration and a powerful pathway to quiet our fears, lift our spirits and give us direction.

I hope Common Sense is Uncommon 2, provides you with a cozy place to turn for encouragement and the words serve as an unexpected conversation starter for everyone.

We often don't know what to say to someone who is hurting, we can't find the words, sharing this book can be a gesture we can make.

Quotes rescue us and the people we love.

Life is a roller coaster of adversity where common sense does not exist... maybe that is why we crave quotes.

Words Matter...this book is an opportunity to celebrate our favourite quotes and help heal us. A bit!

Common Sense Is Uncommon

Helping You Live Up to Your Potential

Anne Balaban

Common Sense Is Uncommon
Helping You Live Up to Your Potential

iUniverse books may be ordered through booksellers or by contacting:

iUniverse
1663 Liberty Drive
Bloomington, IN 47403
www.iuniverse.com
844-349-9409

ISBN: 978-1-4620-2105-5 (sc)
ISBN: 978-1-4620-2106-2 (e)

Library of Congress Control Number: 2011908514

Print information available on the last page.

iUniverse rev. date: 11/03/2022

To David and Steven,
with gratitude and love

WILF,   GOLDIE,
JOEL, JOE,   IRENA, FRAN,
ALEXIA, ANTONETTE, BERNADINE, BIRDIE, BOGDAN,
DOREEN, CYNTHIA, IRENE, JENNIFER, KAREN, LINDA,
MARIANNE, MOMICA GRACE, JACK, STUART, SEAN, ALI, ANDREW,
VANESSA, BARB, LISA, LONNIE, LAURA, LILY, BEV, PHILIP, REVA, FRAN,
PENNY, LORRAINE, ALICE, JESS, RICHARD, JUDY, RAY, SUZANNE,
ANN, JEANIE, MARILYN, ANGIE, HANS, JANE, NORKA, SURELY,
AARON, MARA, IRA, LILY, LOUCAS, SANDY, MICKEY, HEATHER,
MIRIAM, HANNAH, IAN, KENDAL, BOBBY, SOPHIE, JENSEN, REVA,
MARK, LUBA, ALANA, TRACEY, JESSIE, LYNN, FAYE, ALI, LORI, ALLAN,
HELEN, ANDY, SHERRY, TONY, BEN, DIANNE, MARIANNE, NICOLE,
DAISY, LYDIA, YVONNE, CATHERINE, JACK, NEIL, ARLENE, MARK,
SEAN, PAULA, KATHY, AMANDA, HAILEY, HAZEL, AGATA, MARTA,
DONNA, SHEILA, DEBBIE, ROBERT, WILLIAM, BOB, SUSAN,
HENRY, FLORENE, CHUCK, YASMIN, CHRIS, MARLA, ANDREA,
GARY, HOWARD, MITRA, ERIKA, MICHAEL, JOCK. JESS, MITRA,
LLOYD, ANUSHYA, GAIL, JERRY, JEFF, JEANNE, BRIAN,
VANESSA, CAROL, DANIEL, SAUL, DINO, STEPHAN, ISABEL, EDNA MAE,
TIM, DOUG, JOE, ISABEL, DANDRA, GREG, GISELLE, PAUL,
SHAYLA, GAIL, GEOFF, LEILA, SHARON, RUTH, RABIA,
SADAF, SANJAY, IRENE, ARIEL, ARSALAN, CARLA, DON,
MISHAEL. ILYA, ROHANNA, SANI, SASI, AN, ARIEL,
TAIYA, DENZIL, FAYE, MARIA, MICHELLE, NORMA,
PAULINE, URSULA, TONY, YOGESH, CYNTHIA,
KATHARINA, BRENDA, JESS, KELLY,
LYNN, ANNA MARIA, CHEA, MONICA,
MARILYN, CONNIE, MALCOLM,
SAPPHIRE, DIANNE, JOCK,
JOHN, RICK, MONICA,
ANGELA, DAN, LINCOLN,
KELLY, JORDAN.
MARIA, FANNY,
VIOLA

The idea that our feelings are controlled by our thoughts was first introduced by the Greek philosopher Epictetus, when he wrote "it is not things themselves that disturb men, but their judgments about these things." Much later, the playwright William Shakespeare noted how our thoughts determine feelings when he wrote "there is nothing either good or bad, but thinking makes it so."

Since the average person has 60,000 thoughts per day and of these more than 80% are negative, I wanted to develop a simple, realistic, tool for the reader to identify and replace negative thoughts with positive thoughts. It is with this book, that I am committed to improving the quality of how we think and hope that it lends itself easily to being reread and referenced many times throughout a reader's lifetime.

Strive for progress,
not perfection.

A bad attitude is like a flat tire.
If you don't change it,
you'll never go anywhere.

Life is not measured
by the breaths we take,
but by the moments that
take our breath away.

Make your own destiny.
Don't wait for it to come to you,
life is not a rehearsal.

Tell the truth;
there's less to remember.

Maturity is the art of living
in peace with that which
we cannot change.

Every person I work with knows something better than me.
My job is to listen long enough to find it and use it.

Laughter is the shock absorber
that softens and minimizes
the bumps of life.

Wisdom is divided into two parts:
(a) having a great deal to say,
and (b) not saying it.

The grass is always greener
on the other side;
until you jump the fence
and see the weeds up close.

Don't let yesterday's disappointments overshadow tomorrow's achievements.

If you want to change your life,
change your mind.

A word of encouragement during failure is worth more than a whole book of praises after a success.

A lot of people have gone further than they thought they could because someone else thought they could.

The winner always has a plan;
The loser always has an excuse.

I am never a failure until I begin blaming others.

There is no elevator to success.
You must take the stairs.

Work hard in silence, let your success be your noise.

When you feel like quitting think about why you started.

Don't let insecurity ruin the beauty you were born with.

Hard things are put in our way,
not to stop us, but to call out our
courage and strength.

The problem is not the problem;
the problem is your attitude
about the problem.

Be more willing to be impressed
than eager to impress.

We not only need to be willing to give, but also to be open to receiving from others.

Kindness is a language
which the blind can see
and the deaf can hear.

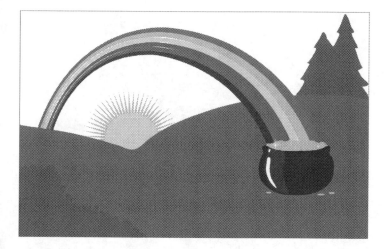

Worry is imagination misplaced.

The truth doesn't cost anything, but a lie could cost you everything.

Good habits are formed;
bad habits we fall into.

Remember yesterday.
Dream of tomorrow.
Live for Today.

Printed in the United States
by Baker & Taylor Publisher Services